How to Use Your Samsung Galaxy S24

A Comprehensive Guide

John Jones

Table Of Contents

INTRODUCTION

Welcome to the Samsung Galaxy S24 user guide. In this guide, you will learn how to use your new Galaxy S24 device, which is one of the most advanced smartphones in the market. The Galaxy S24 series consists of three models: the Galaxy S24, the Galaxy S24 Plus, and the Galaxy S24 Ultra. Each model has its own unique features and specifications, but they all share the same powerful performance, stunning display, and innovative AI capabilities.

In this section, we will cover the following topics:

- About the Galaxy S24 series: Learn more about the main features and differences of the Galaxy S24 models.

- What's in the box: Find out what accessories and items are included with your Galaxy S24 device.
- Device layout and key features: Get familiar with the physical design and buttons of your Galaxy S24 device.

About the Galaxy S24 series

The Galaxy S24 series is the latest flagship smartphone lineup from Samsung, launched on January 17, 2024. The Galaxy S24 series redefines what a smartphone can do, with advanced AI enhancements that take your mobile experience to new heights. You can now search, message, and call in completely new ways that break down language, time, and productivity barriers. You can also transform your social accounts into photographic masterpieces with top-tier cameras that capture images in exceptional quality even in the dark. Plus, you'll find powerful processors across the range, that let you effortlessly switch between multiple apps and deliver the ultimate mobile gaming experience. Paired with a huge battery capacity, you can watch and play all day without worrying about how much juice you have left.

The Galaxy S24 series consists of three models: the Galaxy S24, the Galaxy S24 Plus, and the Galaxy S24 Ultra. The Galaxy S24 is the smallest and most affordable model, with a 6.2-inch FHD+ AMOLED display, 8GB of RAM, and 128GB or 256GB of storage. The Galaxy S24 Plus is the mid-range model, with a 6.7-inch QHD+ AMOLED display, 12GB of RAM, and 256GB or 512GB of storage. The Galaxy S24 Ultra is the premium model, with a 6.8-inch QHD+ AMOLED display, 12GB of RAM, and 256GB, 512GB, or 1TB of storage. The Galaxy S24 Ultra also features a 200MP main camera, a 50MP telephoto camera with 5x optical zoom, and a ProVisual Engine that enhances the image quality and performance.

All three models are powered by either the Qualcomm Snapdragon 8 Gen 3 for Galaxy or the Samsung Exynos 2400 processor, depending on the region. They also support 5G connectivity, wireless charging, reverse wireless charging, and water and dust resistance. They run on Android 14 with Samsung's One UI 4.0 on top, which offers a smooth and intuitive user interface.

What's in the box

When you purchase a Galaxy S24 device, you will find the following items in the box:

- A Galaxy S24 device
- A USB-C charging and data transfer cable
- A SIM ejection tool
- The obligatory paper inserts

Please note that the box does not include a charging brick, headphones, or a protective case. You will need to purchase these accessories separately if you need them.

Alternatively, you can use your existing accessories that are compatible with your Galaxy S24 device.

Device layout and key features

The Galaxy S24 device has a sleek and elegant design, with a metal frame and a glass back. The front of the device is dominated by the edge-to-edge display, which has a small hole-punch cutout for the front-facing camera. The display also has an in-screen fingerprint scanner for biometric security. The back of the device has a rectangular camera module that houses the rear cameras and the LED flash. The device also has a speaker, a microphone, and a USB-C port at the bottom, and a SIM card tray and another microphone at the top. The device does not have a 3.5mm headphone jack, so you will need to use wireless headphones or a USB-C adapter to listen to audio.

The device has three physical buttons on the right side: a power button and a volume rocker. You can press and hold the power button to turn the device on or off, or to access the power menu. You can also double-press the power button to launch the camera app, or press and hold it to activate Bixby, Samsung's virtual assistant. You can adjust the volume by pressing the volume rocker up or down. You can also press and hold the volume down and power buttons together to take a screenshot.

The device has several key features that make it stand out from other smartphones. Some of these features are:

- **Live Translate:** A feature that lets you translate voice calls and text messages in real time, using the power of AI. You can speak and hear in your own language, while the other person speaks and hears in theirs.

- **Note Assist:** A feature that lets you summarize any written content into easy-to-skim bullet points, using the power of AI. You can get a clear overview of what you're reading, without missing any important details.

- **Chat Assist:** A feature that lets you reply to messages faster and easier, using the power of AI. You can get smart suggestions for replies, emojis, stickers, and GIFs, based on the context and tone of the conversation.

- **DeX:** A feature that lets you use your Galaxy S24 device as a desktop computer, by connecting it to a monitor, keyboard, and mouse. You can access all your apps and files on a larger screen, and enjoy a PC-like experience.

- **Wireless Projection:** A feature that lets you mirror your Galaxy S24 device's screen to a compatible TV or monitor, without using any cables. You can watch videos, play games, or give presentations on a bigger screen, wirelessly.

These are some of the topics that you will learn more about in this guide. We hope that you enjoy using your Galaxy S24 device, and that this guide helps you make the most of it.

GETTING STARTED

Before you can start using your Samsung Galaxy S24, you need to perform some basic tasks to set it up. In this section, we will guide you through the following steps:

- Inserting the SIM card and battery
- Charging the device
- Turning the device on and off
- Setting up the device
- Transferring data from your old device

- **Inserting the SIM card and battery**

Your Samsung Galaxy S24 uses a nano-SIM card to connect to your mobile network. You also need to insert a battery to power your device. To insert the SIM card and battery, follow these steps:

- Locate the SIM card tray on the bottom of your device. Use the SIM eject tool or a paper clip to gently push into the small hole next to the tray and pop it out.

- Place your SIM card on the tray with the gold contacts facing down and the cut-off corner aligned with the tray. If you have a dual SIM model, you can place a second SIM card on the other slot of the tray.

- Slide the sim card tray back into the device until it clicks into place.

- Place the battery in your device, top first, matching the battery contacts with the device contacts and press the battery into place.

- **Charging the device**

Your Samsung Galaxy S24 comes with a USB-C cable that you can use to charge your device. You will need to purchase a compatible charger separately, as it is not included in the box. follow these steps to charge your device,:

- Plug the USB-C cable into the charger and the other end into the USB-C port on the bottom of your device.

- Plug the charger into a power outlet and wait for the battery icon to show the charging status. You can also check the battery percentage on the lock screen or the notification panel.

- When the battery is fully charged, unplug the charger and the cable from your device and the power outlet.

Note: Your Samsung Galaxy S24 supports fast charging up to 25W, as well as wireless charging and reverse wireless charging. You will need to use a compatible charger and cable to achieve the fastest charging speeds. You can also use a wireless charger or another device that supports reverse wireless charging to charge your device wirelessly. For more information, see the Advanced Features section of this guide.

- Turning the device on and off

To turn on your Samsung Galaxy S24, press and hold the Side key on the right side of your device for a few seconds. You will see the Samsung logo and a welcome screen. To turn off your device, press and hold the Side key and the Volume down key simultaneously for a few seconds. You will see a power menu with options to power off, restart, or activate emergency mode. Tap Power off to turn off your device. To restart your device, tap Restart. To enter emergency mode, tap Emergency mode and follow the on-screen instructions.

- **Setting up the device**

When you turn on your Samsung Galaxy S24 for the first time, you will need to set up some basic settings and preferences. You can also transfer your data from your old device using Smart Switch or Google Backup. To set up your device, follow these steps:

- Choose your language and tap Start.

- Connect to a Wi-Fi network or use your mobile data. Tap Next.

- Read and agree to the terms and conditions. Tap Next.

- Sign in to your Samsung account or create a new one. You can also skip this step and sign in later. Tap Next.

- Choose your Google services and preferences. Tap Next.

- Sign in to your Google account or create a new one. You can also skip this step and sign in later. Tap Next.

- Set up your biometric security options. You can choose to use face recognition, fingerprint scanner, or both. You will also need to set up a PIN, pattern, or password as a backup. Follow the on-screen instructions to register your face and/or fingerprints. Tap Next.

- Choose your device name and tap Next.

- Choose your device protection options. You can enable Find My Mobile, Google Find My Device, and Send SOS messages. Tap Next.

- Choose your Samsung Cloud options. You can enable Samsung Cloud backup, sync, and restore. Tap Next.

- Choose your Smart Switch options. You can transfer your data from your old device using a wireless or wired connection. Tap Next and follow the on-screen instructions to connect your old device and select the data you want to transfer. Tap Transfer and wait for the process to complete.

- Choose your Google Backup options. You can restore your data from your Google account or set up your device as a new one. Tap Next and follow the on-screen instructions to select the backup you want to restore or skip this step.

- Choose your additional apps and features. You can download and install recommended apps and features from Samsung and Google. Tap Next.

- Choose your Samsung Daily options. You can enable Samsung Daily, a personalized news and content feed on your home screen. Tap Next.

- Choose your Bixby options. You can enable Bixby, Samsung's virtual assistant, and customize its settings. Tap Next.

- Choose your Edge panel options. You can enable Edge panel, a quick access menu for your favorite apps and tools on the edge of your screen. Tap Next.

- Choose your navigation options. You can choose to use navigation buttons or navigation gestures to navigate your device. Tap Next.

- Choose your theme options. You can choose a theme for your device, including wallpaper, icons, and fonts. Tap Next.

- Tap Finish to complete the setup process.

Transferring data from your old device

If you did not transfer your data from your old device during the setup process, you can still do it later using Smart Switch or Google Backup. Smart Switch lets you transfer data from most Android or iOS devices, and even some older Windows and Blackberry devices. Google Backup lets you restore data from your Google account. To transfer data from your old device, follow these steps:

- Open the Smart Switch app on your Samsung Galaxy S24. If you don't have it, you can download it from the Play Store or the Galaxy Store.

- Tap Send data on your old device and tap Receive data on your new device. Check the OS of your old device and choose the appropriate source. Select Wireless or Cable depending on how you want to connect your devices.

- Open Smart Switch on your old device to connect, and then tap Allow to allow the connection on your old device. Select the data you want to transfer, and then tap

Transfer at the bottom right. Wait for the process to complete, and then tap Done on both devices.

- Alternatively, you can open the Settings app on your Samsung Galaxy S24 and tap Accounts and backup. Tap Backup and restore, and then tap Restore data. Select the Google account you want to restore from, and then select the data you want to restore. Tap Restore at the bottom right. Wait for the process to complete, and then tap Done.

BASIC OPERATIONS

The Samsung Galaxy S24 is a powerful and versatile smartphone that lets you do more with your device. In this section, we will explain how to use the basic functions and features of your Galaxy S24, such as:

- Using the touchscreen and gestures
- Using the home screen and app screen
- Using the notification panel and quick settings
- Using the edge screen and edge panel
- Using the navigation bar and navigation gestures
- Using the lock screen and biometric security
- Using the Samsung account and cloud services

- **Using the touchscreen and gestures**

Your Galaxy S24 has a touchscreen that responds to your touch and gestures. You can perform various actions with your fingers, such as tapping, swiping, pinching, and zooming. Here are some common gestures and their functions:

- Tap: Touch the screen lightly with your finger to select an item, open an app, or confirm an action.

- Double tap: Tap the screen twice quickly to zoom in or out on an image or a web page, or to wake up or turn off the screen.

- Swipe: Swipe your finger across the screen to scroll through a list, move to the next or previous screen, or unlock the device.

- Drag: Touch and hold an item, and then move your finger to move it to another location.

- Pinch: Touch the screen with two fingers and spread them apart or bring them together to zoom in or out on an image or a web page.

- Rotate: Touch the screen with two fingers and rotate them clockwise or counterclockwise to rotate an image or a web page.

- Long press: Touch and hold an item for a few seconds to access more options or functions.

- Flick: Swipe your finger quickly across the screen to scroll through a list or a web page faster.

You can also use Circle to Search with Google, a new feature that lets you search anything on your screen by drawing a ring around it. To use this feature, follow these steps:

- Touch and hold the Home button to activate Google Assistant.

- Draw a circle around the item you want to search, such as a word, a phrase, an image, or a location.

- Google Assistant will show you relevant information and results from the web, such as definitions, translations, images, videos, maps, and more.

- You can tap on the results to open them in the browser, or swipe up to see more options and actions.

- **Using the home screen and app screen**

The home screen is where you can access your favorite apps, widgets, and shortcuts. The app screen is where you can find all the apps installed on your phone. You can customize the layout, theme, and wallpaper of your home screen and app screen.

To access the home screen, press the Home button or swipe up from the bottom of the screen. To access the app screen, swipe up from the home screen or tap the Apps icon at the bottom right. To return to the home screen from the app screen, press the Home button or swipe down from the top of the screen.

You can add, remove, or rearrange the apps and widgets on your home screen and app screen. To do this, follow these steps:

- Touch and hold an empty space on the home screen or app screen to enter the editing mode.

- To add an app or a widget, tap the Add icon at the bottom left, and then select the app or widget you want to add. Drag it to the desired location on the screen and release it.

- To remove an app or a widget, touch and hold it, and then drag it to the Remove icon at the top of the screen and release it.

- To rearrange an app or a widget, touch and hold it, and then drag it to the desired location on the screen and release it. You can also move it to another screen by dragging it to the edge of the screen.

- To create a folder, touch and hold an app, and then drag it over another app and release it. A folder will be created with the two apps inside. You can add more apps to the folder by dragging them over it. You can also rename the folder by tapping on its name and entering a new one.

- To exit the editing mode, press the Home button or tap anywhere outside the screen.

You can also change the theme and wallpaper of your home screen and app screen. To do this, follow these steps:

- Touch and hold an empty space on the home screen or app screen to enter the editing mode.

- Tap the Wallpaper icon at the bottom right to change the wallpaper. You can choose from the preloaded wallpapers, or select your own photos or images from the gallery or the cloud. You can also apply different effects and filters to the wallpaper. Tap Set as wallpaper to apply the changes.

- Tap the Themes icon at the bottom right to change the theme. You can choose from the preloaded themes, or download more themes from the Galaxy Store or the Google Play Store. A theme can change the

appearance of your icons, fonts, colors, and sounds. Tap Apply to apply the changes.

- To exit the editing mode, press the Home button or tap anywhere outside the screen.

- **Using the notification panel and quick settings**

The notification panel shows your incoming notifications, such as messages, calls, and alerts. You can swipe down from the top of the screen to open it. The quick settings panel lets you access frequently used settings and apps, such as Wi-Fi, Bluetooth, and flashlight. You can swipe down again from the notification panel or swipe down with two fingers to open it. You can also customize the quick settings buttons and layout.

To use the notification panel, follow these steps:

- Swipe down from the top of the screen to open the notification panel.

- To view more details about a notification, tap on it. You can also swipe left or right on a notification to dismiss it, or swipe down on it to expand it and access more options and actions.

- To clear all notifications, tap the Clear icon at the bottom right of the panel.

- To access the quick settings panel, swipe down again from the notification panel or swipe down with two fingers from the top of the screen.

To use the quick settings panel, follow these steps:

- Swipe down from the top of the screen with two fingers to open the quick settings panel.

- To turn on or off a setting or an app, tap on its icon. You can also touch and hold an icon to access more options and settings.

- To rearrange the quick settings buttons, tap the Edit icon at the bottom left of the panel. You can drag and drop the buttons to change their order or location. You can also add or remove buttons by tapping the Add icon or the Remove icon. Tap Done to save the changes.

- To change the layout of the quick settings panel, tap the Layout icon at the bottom right of the panel. You can choose from different grid sizes and shapes for the buttons. Tap Apply to save the changes.

- **Using the edge screen and edge panel**

The edge screen is a curved part of the display that extends beyond the main screen. The edge panel is a quick access menu for your favorite apps and tools that you can access from the edge screen. You can customize the edge panel and its contents.

To access the edge panel, follow these steps:

- Swipe in from the edge of the screen where the edge panel handle is located. You can change the position and size of the edge panel handle in the settings.

- To switch between different edge panels, swipe left or right on the edge panel. You can also tap the indicator icons at the bottom of the edge panel to jump to a specific panel.

- To use an edge panel, tap on the app or tool you want to use. You can also touch and hold an app or tool to access more options and settings.

- To close the edge panel, swipe out from the edge of the screen or tap anywhere outside the edge panel.

To customize the edge panel, follow these steps:

- Swipe in from the edge of the screen to open the edge panel.

- Tap the Settings icon at the bottom left of the edge panel to enter the settings menu.

- To add or remove edge panels, tap the Panels icon at the top of the menu. You can select or deselect the edge panels you want to use. You can also download more edge panels from the Galaxy Store or the Google Play Store.

- To rearrange the edge panels, tap the Reorder icon at the top of the menu. You can drag and drop the edge panels to change their order or location.

- To change the edge panel handle, tap the Handle icon at the top of the menu. You can change the position, size, transparency, and color of the edge panel handle.

- To exit the settings menu, tap the Back icon at the top left of the menu or tap anywhere outside the menu.

- **Using the navigation bar and navigation gestures**

The navigation bar is a row of buttons at the bottom of the screen that lets you navigate your device. The navigation bar consists of three buttons: the Back button, the Home button, and the Recents button. The Back button lets you go back to the previous screen or app. The Home button lets you go to the home screen or activate Google Assistant. The Recents button lets you view and switch between recently used apps.

The navigation gestures are a set of swipe actions that let you navigate your device without using the navigation bar. You can swipe up from the bottom of the screen to go to the home screen, swipe up and hold to view the recent apps, or swipe from the left or right edge of the screen to go back.

You can choose to use the navigation gestures instead of the navigation bar. To do this, follow these steps:

- Open the Settings app and tap Display.

- Scroll down and tap the Navigation bar.

- Tap Swipe gestures to enable the navigation gestures.

- Tap More options to customize the navigation gestures. You can choose between Swipe from bottom and Swipe from sides and bottom, depending on how you want to swipe to go back. You can also adjust the Back gesture sensitivity and the Gesture hints.

- To use the navigation gestures, swipe up from the bottom of the screen to go to the home screen, swipe up and hold to view the recent apps, or swipe from the left or right edge of the screen to go back.

- **Using the lock screen and biometric security**

The lock screen is the first screen you see when you turn on or wake up your Galaxy S24. The lock screen shows the date, time, weather, and notifications. You can also access some quick features from the lock screen, such as the camera, the flashlight, and the music player. You can customize the lock screen wallpaper, clock style, and widgets.

To access the lock screen, press the Power button or double tap the screen when the device is off or asleep. To unlock the device, swipe up from the bottom of the screen or use your biometric security method. You can also use the FaceWidgets to access some useful information and controls from the lock screen, such as the alarm, the calendar, and the weather. To use the FaceWidgets, swipe left or right on the clock area of the lock screen.

To customize the lock screen, follow these steps:

- Open the Settings app and tap Lock screen.

- Tap Wallpaper to change the lock screen wallpaper. You can choose from the preloaded wallpapers, or select your own photos or images from the gallery or the cloud. You can also apply different effects and filters to the wallpaper. Tap Set as wallpaper to apply the changes.

- Tap Clock style to change the lock screen clock style. You can choose from different types, colors, and sizes of clocks. You can also add or remove items on the lock screen, such as the date, the battery percentage, and the face recognition icon. Tap Done to apply the changes.

- Tap Widgets to change the lock screen widgets. You can choose which widgets to show on the lock screen, such as the music player, the weather, and the routines. You can also reorder the widgets by dragging and dropping them. Tap Done to apply the changes.

- Tap FaceWidgets to change the FaceWidgets settings. You can choose which FaceWidgets to show on the lock screen, such as the alarm, the calendar, and the weather. You can also reorder the FaceWidgets by dragging and dropping them. You can also enable or disable the option to show the FaceWidgets on the

Always On Display. Tap Done to apply the changes.

- Tap Contact information to add or edit your contact information on the lock screen. You can enter your name, phone number, email address, or any other information you want to display. Tap Save to apply the changes.

- Tap Notifications to change the lock screen notifications settings. You can choose which apps to show notifications on the lock screen, and how to display them. You can also enable or disable the option to wake the screen when you receive a notification. Tap Done to apply the changes.

- Tap App shortcuts to change the lock screen app shortcuts. You can choose which apps to show on the bottom corners of the lock screen, and how to access them. You can also enable or disable the option to launch the camera by double pressing the

Power button. Tap Done to apply the changes.

Your Galaxy S24 supports biometric security methods, such as face recognition and fingerprint scanner, to unlock your device and verify your identity. You can also use a PIN, pattern, or password as a backup method. You can set up and manage your biometric security methods in the Settings app.

To set up and use the face recognition, follow these steps:

- Open the Settings app and tap Biometrics and security.

- Tap Face recognition and enter your PIN, pattern, or password to confirm.

- Tap Continue and follow the on-screen instructions to register your face. Make sure your face is fully visible and centered in the circle. You can also enable or disable the option to require open eyes for face recognition. Tap Done to complete the registration.

- To unlock your device with face recognition, turn on or wake up your device and look at the front camera. You will see a face recognition icon on the lock screen. When your face is recognized, the device will be unlocked.

- To use face recognition for other purposes, such as signing in to apps or verifying payments, you can enable or disable the option to use face recognition for each app or service in the Settings app.

To set up and use the fingerprint scanner, follow these steps:

- Open the Settings app and tap Biometrics and security.

- Tap Fingerprint scanner and enter your PIN, pattern, or password to confirm.

- Tap Continue and follow the on-screen instructions to register your fingerprint. Place your finger on the fingerprint scanner area on the screen and lift it when you feel a vibration. Repeat this process until the registration is complete. You can register up to four fingerprints. Tap Done to complete the registration.

- To unlock your device with the fingerprint scanner, turn on or wake up your device and place your finger on the fingerprint scanner area on the screen. You will see a fingerprint icon on the lock screen. When your fingerprint is recognized, the device will be unlocked.

- To use the fingerprint scanner for other purposes, such as signing in to apps or verifying payments, you can enable or disable the option to use the fingerprint

scanner for each app or service in the
Settings app.

- **Using the Samsung account and
  cloud services**

Your Samsung account is your gateway to all
things Samsung. You can use your Samsung
account to access and sync your data across
your Samsung devices, such as contacts,
calendar, notes, photos, and more. You can
also use your Samsung account to access
various Samsung services and apps, such as
Samsung Cloud, Samsung Pay, Samsung
Health, Samsung Members, and more.

To create and sign in to your Samsung
account, follow these steps:

- Open the Settings app and tap Accounts
and backup.

- Tap Accounts and then tap Add account.

- Tap Samsung account and then tap Create account or Sign in.

- Follow the on-screen instructions to enter your email address, password, and personal information. You can also sign in with your Google or Facebook account. Tap Agree to accept the terms and conditions.

- Tap Done to complete the sign-in process.

To manage your Samsung account settings and preferences, follow these steps:

- Open the Settings app and tap Accounts and backup.

- Tap Accounts and then tap Samsung account.

- Tap your email address at the top of the screen to access your Samsung account profile. You can edit your profile information, change your password, manage your devices, and more.

- Tap the menu icon at the top right of the screen to access more Samsung account options. You can view your Samsung account benefits, check your Samsung account storage, manage your Samsung account security, and more.

Samsung Cloud is a cloud service that lets you back up, sync, and restore your data across your Samsung devices. You can use Samsung Cloud to store your contacts, calendar, notes, photos, videos, and more. You can also use Samsung Cloud to sync your settings, apps, and home screen layout across your devices. You can access Samsung Cloud from the Settings app or the Gallery app.

To use Samsung Cloud, follow these steps:

- Open the Settings app and tap Accounts and backup.

- Tap Samsung Cloud and sign in to your Samsung account if prompted.

- Tap Backup and restore to manage your backup and restore settings. You can choose which data to back up to Samsung Cloud, and when to back up automatically or manually. You can also choose which data to restore from Samsung Cloud, and select the device you want to restore from.

- Tap Sync and auto backup settings to manage your sync and auto backup settings. You can choose which data to sync across your devices, and when to sync automatically or manually. You can also choose which settings, apps, and home screen layout to sync across your devices.

- Tap Samsung Cloud Drive to access your Samsung Cloud Drive. You can view, upload, download, or delete your files stored in Samsung Cloud Drive. You can also create folders and share your files with others.

- Tap Gallery to access your Samsung Cloud Gallery. You can view, upload, download, or delete your photos and videos stored in Samsung Cloud Gallery. You can also create albums and share your photos and videos with others.

These are some of the basic operations and features of your Samsung Galaxy S24. You can learn more about the advanced features and settings of your device in the next sections of this guide.

COMMUNICATION

Your Samsung Galaxy S24 lets you communicate with your friends, family, and colleagues in various ways. You can make and receive calls, send and receive messages, set up and use email accounts, and use social media and instant messaging apps. In this section, we will explain how to use these communication features on your Galaxy S24, such as:

- Making and receiving calls
- Sending and receiving messages
- Setting up and using email accounts
- Using social media and instant messaging apps

- **Making and receiving calls**

You can use the Phone app to make and receive voice and video calls on your Galaxy S24. You can also use the Contacts app to manage your contacts and call logs. You can customize the call settings and features, such as call blocking, call forwarding, and call waiting.

To make a call, follow these steps:

- Open the Phone app and tap the Keypad icon at the bottom of the screen.

- Enter the phone number you want to call, or tap the Contacts icon to select a contact from your contacts list.

- Tap the Phone icon to make a voice call, or tap the Video icon to make a video call. You can also tap the Menu icon to access more options, such as adding a call, sending a message, or viewing the contact details.

- To end the call, tap the End icon.

To receive a call, follow these steps:

- When you receive an incoming call, you will see the caller's name, number, and photo on the screen. You can also see the call type, such as voice or video, and the call duration.

- To answer the call, swipe the Answer icon to the right. You can also swipe the Video icon to the right to answer as a video call.

- To reject the call, swipe the Reject icon to the left. You can also swipe the Message icon to the left to reject the call and send a quick message to the caller.

- To silence the ringtone, press the Volume down button or the Power button.

To manage your call settings and features, follow these steps:

- Open the Phone app and tap the Menu icon at the top right of the screen.

- Tap Settings to access the call settings menu. You can change various settings and features, such as:

  - Block numbers: You can block unwanted calls from specific numbers or unknown callers. You can also view and manage your blocked numbers list.

  - Caller ID and spam protection: You can enable or disable the caller ID and spam protection feature, which helps you identify and avoid spam calls. You can also report spam numbers or mark them as not spam.

  - Call forwarding: You can forward your incoming calls to another number or device. You can choose to forward all calls, or only when busy, unanswered, or unreachable.

- Call waiting: You can enable or disable the call waiting feature, which lets you receive another call while you are on a call. You can choose to answer, reject, or hold the second call.

- Voicemail: You can set up and access your voicemail service. You can choose your voicemail provider, number, and settings. You can also listen to your voicemail messages and delete them.

- Wi-Fi calling: You can enable or disable the Wi-Fi calling feature, which lets you make and receive calls over a Wi-Fi network instead of a cellular network. You can choose your preferred network for calls, and manage your emergency address.

- **Sending and receiving messages**

You can use the Messages app to send and receive text messages (SMS) and multimedia messages (MMS) on your

Galaxy S24. You can also use the Chat features to send and receive enhanced messages (RCS) with other compatible devices. You can customize the messages settings and features, such as notifications, themes, and spam protection.

To send a message, follow these steps:

- Open the Messages app and tap the Compose icon at the bottom right of the screen.

- Enter the recipient's phone number or name, or tap the Contacts icon to select a contact from your contacts list. You can also add multiple recipients to create a group conversation.

- Enter your message in the text field, or tap the Microphone icon to use voice input. You can also tap the Emoji icon to add emojis, stickers, or GIFs, or tap the Plus icon to add attachments, such as photos, videos, audio, location, or contacts.

- Tap the Send icon to send your message. You can also tap the Arrow icon to send your message as a scheduled message, which will be sent at a later time or date that you choose.

- To delete a message, touch and hold it, and then tap the Delete icon at the top of the screen. You can also select multiple messages to delete them at once.

To receive a message, follow these steps:

- When you receive a new message, you will see a notification on the screen. You can also see the message count on the Messages app icon.

- To view the message, swipe down from the top of the screen to open the notification panel, and then tap the message notification. You can also open the Messages app and tap the conversation you want to view.

- To reply to the message, enter your message in the text field, or use the same steps as sending a message. You can also swipe left or right on the message to access more options, such as calling, copying, or forwarding the message.

- To mark the message as read or unread, touch and hold it, and then tap the Mark as read or Mark as unread icon at the top of the screen. You can also select multiple messages to mark them as read or unread at once.

To manage your messages settings and features, follow these steps:

- Open the Messages app and tap the Menu icon at the top right of the screen.

- Tap Settings to access the messages settings menu. You can change various settings and features, such as:

- Notifications: You can enable or disable the message notifications, and customize the notification sound, vibration, and style. You can also enable or disable the notification badges, which show the message count on the app icon.

- Chat features: You can enable or disable the chat features, which let you send and receive enhanced messages (RCS) with other compatible devices. You can also manage your chat features settings, such as read receipts, typing indicators, and data usage.

- Themes: You can change the theme of the Messages app, including the background, bubble style, and font size. You can choose from the preloaded themes, or select your own photos or images from the gallery or the cloud.

- Spam protection: You can enable or disable the spam protection feature, which helps you identify and avoid spam messages. You can also report spam messages or mark them as not spam.

- Blocked contacts: You can block unwanted messages from specific numbers or unknown senders. You can also view and manage your blocked contacts list.

- Advanced: You can access more messages settings, such as auto-delete old messages, group messaging, emergency alerts, and SIM card messages.

- **Setting up and using email accounts**

You can use the Email app to set up and use your email accounts on your Galaxy S24.

You can add multiple email accounts from different providers, such as Gmail, Outlook, Yahoo, and more. You can also sync your email data, such as contacts, calendar, and notes, across your devices. You can customize the email settings and features, such as notifications, signatures, and spam filters.

To set up an email account, follow these steps:

- Open the Email app and tap the Menu icon at the top left of the screen.

- Tap the Add account icon at the bottom right of the screen.

- Enter your email address and password, or tap the Manual setup icon to enter your email settings manually. You can also tap the Google icon to add a Gmail account, or tap the Other icon to add another email account.

- Tap Sign in or Next to complete the setup process. You can also enable or disable the sync options for your email account, such as contacts, calendar, and notes.

- To add another email account, repeat the same steps.

To use an email account, follow these steps:

- Open the Email app and tap the Menu icon at the top left of the screen.

- Tap the email account you want to use, or tap the All accounts icon to view all your email accounts at once.

- To compose a new email, tap the Compose icon at the bottom right of the screen. Enter the recipient's email address or name, or tap the Contacts icon to select a contact from your contacts list. You can also add multiple recipients to create a group email. Enter the subject and the message in the text fields, or tap the Microphone icon to use voice input. You can also tap the Attach icon to add attachments, such as photos, videos, audio, documents, or contacts. Tap the Send icon to send your email. You can also tap the Menu icon to access more options, such as adding a signature, requesting a read receipt, or scheduling the email to be sent later.

- To view an email, tap the email you want to view from the inbox or another folder. You can also swipe left or right on the email to access more options, such as marking as read, deleting, or archiving the email.

- To reply to an email, tap the Reply icon at the bottom of the screen. You can also tap the Reply all icon to reply to all the recipients, or tap the Forward icon to forward the email to another recipient. You can use the same steps as composing a new email to enter your reply or forward message. Tap the Send icon to send your reply or forward message.

- To delete an email, touch and hold the email, and then tap the Delete icon at the top of the screen. You can also select multiple emails.

- **Using social media and instant messaging apps**

You can use various social media and instant messaging apps on your Galaxy S24 to stay connected with your friends, family, and followers. You can download and install these apps from the Play Store or the Galaxy Store, such as Facebook, Instagram, Twitter, WhatsApp, Telegram, and more. You can also sync your contacts and accounts across these apps, and customize the app settings and features, such as notifications, themes, and privacy.

To use social media and instant messaging apps, follow these steps:

- Open the Play Store or the Galaxy Store app and search for the app you want to use. You can also browse the categories or recommendations to find the app you want.

- Tap the app you want to use and then tap Install to download and install the app on your device. You may need to grant some permissions and accept some terms and conditions to use the app.

- Open the app and sign in to your account or create a new one. You may need to enter your phone number, email address, or other information to verify your identity. You can also sign in with your Google or Facebook account if the app supports it.

- To use the app, follow the app's instructions and features. You can usually send and receive messages, photos, videos, audio, stickers, GIFs, and more. You can also create or join groups, channels, stories, and live streams. You can also like, comment, share, and follow other users and content.

- To manage your app settings and features, tap the Menu icon or the Settings icon in the app. You can change various settings and features, such as notifications, themes, privacy, security, data usage, and more.

These are some of the communication features and settings of your Samsung Galaxy S24. You can learn more about the internet and network features and settings of your device in the next sections of this guide.

INTERNET AND NETWORK

Your Samsung Galaxy S24 lets you connect to the internet and network in various ways. You can use Wi-Fi and mobile data to access online services and apps, such as web browsing, email, social media, and more. You can also use the hotspot and tethering features to share your internet connection with other devices, such as laptops, tablets, and smart TVs. You can also use the VPN and private mode features to enhance your online privacy and security.

In this section, we will explain how to use these internet and network features on your Galaxy S24, such as:

- Connecting to Wi-Fi and mobile data

- Using the web browser and bookmarks
- Using the hotspot and tethering features
- Using the VPN and private mode features

- **Connecting to Wi-Fi and mobile data**

You can use Wi-Fi and mobile data to connect to the internet and network on your Galaxy S24. Wi-Fi is a wireless network that uses radio waves to transmit data. Mobile data is a cellular network that uses cellular towers to transmit data. You can choose which network to use depending on your location, availability, and preference. You can also switch between networks automatically or manually.

To connect to Wi-Fi, follow these steps:

- Open the Settings app and tap Connections.

- Tap Wi-Fi and then tap the switch to turn it on.

- Tap the Wi-Fi network you want to connect to, or tap Add network to enter the network name and password manually. You may need to enter some additional information, such as the security type, the IP address, or the proxy settings, depending on the network.

- Tap Connect to join the network. You will see a Wi-Fi icon on the status bar when you are connected.

- To disconnect from the network, tap the network name and then tap Forget. You can also turn off the Wi-Fi switch to turn off Wi-Fi completely.

To connect to mobile data, follow these steps:

- Open the Settings app and tap Connections.

- Tap Data usage and then tap the switch to turn it on.

- Tap Mobile networks and then tap Network mode. You can choose which network mode to use, such as 5G, 4G, 3G, or 2G, depending on your network provider and coverage. You can also choose to use 5G only when needed, or always use 5G when available.

- Tap Network operators and then tap Select automatically or Select manually. You can choose which network operator to use, depending on your network provider and roaming status. You can also search for available networks and select the one you want to use.

- Tap Access point names and then tap Add or Edit. You can enter or modify the access point name (APN) settings, which are the settings that allow your device to connect to the mobile data network. You may need to get these settings from your network provider or online.

- Tap Save to apply the changes. You will see a mobile data icon on the status bar when you are connected.

- To disconnect from the network, turn off the data usage switch to turn off mobile data completely.

To switch between Wi-Fi and mobile data, follow these steps:

- Open the Settings app and tap Connections.

- Tap Wi-Fi and then tap the switch to turn it on or off.

- Tap Data usage and then tap the switch to turn it on or off.

- Alternatively, you can swipe down from the top of the screen to open the quick settings panel, and then tap the Wi-Fi icon or the mobile data icon to turn them on or off.

- You can also enable the Smart network switch feature, which automatically switches between Wi-Fi and mobile data depending on the network quality and availability. To enable this feature, open the Settings app, tap Connections, tap Wi-Fi, tap Advanced, and then tap the switch next to Smart network switch.

- **Using the web browser and bookmarks**

You can use the web browser to access the internet and browse the web on your Galaxy S24. You can use the Samsung Internet app, which is the default web browser, or download and install another web browser from the Play Store or the Galaxy Store, such as Chrome, Firefox, or Opera. You can also use the bookmarks feature to save and manage your favorite web pages.

To use the web browser, follow these steps:

- Open the Samsung Internet app or another web browser app on your device.

- Tap the address bar at the top of the screen and enter the web address or the search term you want to visit or search. You can also tap the Microphone icon to use voice input, or tap the QR code icon to scan a QR code.

- Tap the Go icon or the Search icon to load the web page or the search results. You can also tap the Menu icon to access more options, such as refreshing, sharing, or printing the web page.

- To navigate the web page, swipe up or down to scroll, or swipe left or right to go back or forward. You can also double tap or pinch to zoom in or out, or rotate your device to switch between portrait and landscape mode.

- To open a new tab, tap the Tabs icon at the bottom of the screen and then tap the Plus icon. You can also swipe left or right on the address bar to switch between tabs, or swipe up or down on the tabs icon to view all your tabs. You can also touch and hold a link on a web page and then tap Open in new tab to open it in a new tab.

- To close a tab, tap the Tabs icon at the bottom of the screen and then tap the Close icon on the tab you want to close. You can also swipe left or right on the tab to close it, or tap the Close all icon to close all tabs.

To use the bookmarks, follow these steps:

- To bookmark a web page, tap the Menu icon at the top of the screen and then tap Add bookmark. You can enter or edit the bookmark name and the bookmark folder. Tap Save to add the bookmark.

- To view your bookmarks, tap the Bookmarks icon at the bottom of the screen. You can see all your bookmarks organized by folders. You can also tap the History icon to see your browsing history, or tap the Saved pages icon to see your offline pages.

- To open a bookmark, tap the bookmark you want to open. You can also touch and hold a bookmark to access more options, such as editing, deleting, or sharing the bookmark.

- To manage your bookmarks, tap the Menu icon at the top of the screen and then tap Edit. You can select multiple bookmarks to move, delete, or share them. You can also create, rename, or delete bookmark folders. Tap Done to apply the changes.

- **Using the hotspot and tethering features**

You can use the hotspot and tethering features to share your internet connection with other devices, such as laptops, tablets, and smart TVs. You can share your Wi-Fi or mobile data connection using Wi-Fi hotspot, USB tethering, or Bluetooth tethering. You can customize the hotspot and tethering settings and features, such as network name, password, and data limit.

To use the hotspot and tethering features, follow these steps:

- Open the Settings app and tap Connections.

- Tap Mobile hotspot and tethering and then tap the switch to turn it on.

- Tap Mobile hotspot to share your internet connection using Wi-Fi hotspot. You can change the network name, password, and security type of your hotspot. You can also enable or disable the option to allow all devices to connect, or to turn off the hotspot automatically when no devices are connected. You can also set a data limit for your hotspot usage. Tap Save to apply the changes.

- Tap USB tethering to share your internet connection using USB tethering. You will need to connect your device to another device using a USB cable. You can also enable or disable the option to allow tethering only when the device is plugged in. You can also set a data limit for your tethering usage. Tap Save to apply the changes.

- Tap Bluetooth tethering to share your internet connection using Bluetooth tethering. You will need to pair your device with another device using Bluetooth. You can also enable or disable the option to allow tethering only when the device is plugged in. You can also set a data limit for your tethering usage. Tap Save to apply the changes.

- To connect another device to your hotspot or tethering, follow the instructions on the other device to scan and join your network. You may need to enter the network name and password, or pair the devices using Bluetooth. You will see a hotspot or tethering icon on the status bar when you are connected.

- **Using the VPN and private mode features**

You can use the VPN and private mode features to enhance your online privacy and security on your Galaxy S24. VPN stands for virtual private network, which is a service that creates a secure and encrypted connection between your device and another network. Private mode is a feature that lets you browse the web without leaving any traces, such as history, cookies, or cache.

To use the VPN feature, follow these steps:

- Open the Settings app and tap Connections.

- Tap More connection settings and then tap VPN.

- Tap Add VPN network to add a VPN network. You can choose from the preloaded VPN networks, or enter the VPN settings manually. You may need to get these settings from your VPN provider or online. Tap Save to add the VPN network.

- Tap the VPN network you want to use and then tap Connect. You may need to enter your username and password, or scan a QR code, depending on the VPN network. You will see a VPN icon on the status bar when you are connected.

- To disconnect from the VPN network, tap the VPN network and then tap Disconnect. You can also turn off the VPN switch to turn off VPN completely.

To use the private mode feature, follow these steps:

- Open the Samsung Internet app or another web browser app on your device.

- Tap the Menu icon at the top right of the screen and then tap Turn on private mode. You will see a mask icon on the status bar when you are in private mode.

- To browse the web in private mode, enter the web address or the search term you want to visit or search in the address bar. You can also use the same steps as browsing the web in normal mode to navigate the web pages.

- To exit the private mode, tap the Menu icon at the top right of the screen and then tap Turn off private mode. You can also turn off the private mode switch in the quick settings panel.

MEDIA

Your Samsung Galaxy S24 lets you enjoy various media content on your device. You can take photos and videos with the camera, edit them with the gallery, play them with the media player, stream them with the online services, and enhance them with the Dolby Atmos and AKG sound features. In this section, we will explain how to use these media features on your Galaxy S24, such as:

- Taking photos and videos with the camera
- Editing photos and videos with the gallery
- Playing music and videos with the media player
- Streaming music and videos with the online services
- Using the Dolby Atmos and AKG sound features

- **Taking photos and videos with the camera**

You can use the Camera app to take photos and videos with your Galaxy S24. You can use the rear camera or the front camera, depending on the mode and the angle you want. You can also use various modes and features to enhance your photos and videos, such as night mode, portrait mode, pro mode, slow motion, hyperlapse, and more. You can also customize the camera settings and features, such as resolution, timer, grid lines, and voice control.

To take a photo, follow these steps:

- Open the Camera app and tap the Camera icon at the bottom of the screen.

- Choose the camera you want to use, either the rear camera or the front camera, by tapping the Switch camera icon at the top of the screen. You can also swipe up or down on the screen to switch cameras.

- Choose the mode you want to use, either the photo mode or the video mode, by tapping the Mode icon at the bottom of the screen. You can also swipe left or right on the screen to switch modes. You can see the available modes at the bottom of the screen, such as night mode, portrait mode, pro mode, and more. You can also tap the More icon to access more modes, such as slow motion, hyperlapse, and more.

- Adjust the zoom level by tapping the Zoom icon at the bottom of the screen. You can choose from different zoom levels, such as 0.5x, 1x, 2x, 4x, 10x, and more. You can also pinch to zoom in or out on the screen.

- Adjust the focus and exposure by tapping the screen where you want to focus. You can also drag the brightness slider up or down to adjust the exposure level.

- Tap the Shutter icon to take a photo. You can also press the Volume button or the Power button to take a photo. You can also use the voice control feature to take a photo by saying "Cheese", "Smile", "Capture", or "Shoot".

- To view the photo, tap the Preview icon at the bottom right of the screen. You can also swipe left on the screen to view the photo. You can also edit, share, or delete the photo from the preview screen.

To take a video, follow these steps:

- Open the Camera app and tap the Camera icon at the bottom of the screen.

- Choose the camera you want to use, either the rear camera or the front camera, by tapping the Switch camera icon at the top of the screen. You can also swipe up or down on the screen to switch cameras.

- Choose the video mode by tapping the Mode icon at the bottom of the screen. You can also swipe left or right on the screen to switch modes. You can see the available modes at the bottom of the screen, such as normal video, pro video, super steady, and more. You can also tap the More icon to access more modes, such as slow motion, hyperlapse, and more.

- Adjust the zoom level by tapping the Zoom icon at the bottom of the screen. You can choose from different zoom levels, such as 0.5x, 1x, 2x, 4x, 10x, and more. You can also pinch to zoom in or out on the screen.

- Adjust the focus and exposure by tapping the screen where you want to focus. You can also drag the brightness slider up or down to adjust the exposure level.

- Tap the Record icon to start recording a video. You can also press the Volume button or the Power button to start recording a video. You can also use the voice control feature to start recording a video by saying "Record video".

- To pause the recording, tap the Pause icon. To resume the recording, tap the Record icon again. To stop the recording, tap the Stop icon. You can also press the Volume button or the Power button to stop recording a video. You can also use the voice control feature to stop recording a video by saying "Stop recording".

- To view the video, tap the Preview icon at the bottom right of the screen. You can also swipe left on the screen to view the video. You can also edit, share, or delete the video from the preview screen.

To manage your camera settings and features, follow these steps:

- Open the Camera app and tap the Settings icon at the top left of the screen.

- Tap the Rear camera or the Front camera to access the camera settings for each camera. You can change various settings and features, such as:

- Picture size: You can choose the resolution and aspect ratio of your photos, such as 200MP, 108MP, 40MP, 12MP, and more. You can also choose the format of your photos, such as JPEG or HEIF.

- Video size: You can choose the resolution and frame rate of your videos, such as 8K, 4K, FHD, HD, and more. You can also choose the format of your videos, such as MP4 or HEVC.

- Timer: You can set a timer for your photos and videos, such as 2 seconds, 5 seconds, or 10 seconds.

- Grid lines: You can enable or disable the grid lines on the screen, which help you align your shots. You can choose from different types of grid lines, such as 3x3, 4x4, or square.

- Voice control: You can enable or disable the voice control feature, which lets you take photos and videos by saying voice commands, such as "Cheese", "Smile", "Capture", "Shoot", "Record video", or "Stop recording".

- Shooting methods: You can choose which buttons to use to take photos and videos, such as the Volume button, the Power button, or the floating shutter button. You can also enable or disable the palm gesture, which lets you take a photo by showing your palm to the camera.

- **Editing photos and videos with the gallery**

You can use the Gallery app to view and edit your photos and videos on your Galaxy S24. You can also use the gallery to organize your photos and videos into albums, stories, and collections. You can also sync your photos and videos with Samsung Cloud or Google Photos, and share them with other apps and devices.

To view a photo or a video, follow these steps:

- Open the Gallery app and tap the photo or video you want to view. You can also swipe left or right on the screen to view the previous or next photo or video.

- To zoom in or out on a photo or video, double tap or pinch on the screen. You can also rotate your device to switch between portrait and landscape mode.

- To play a video, tap the Play icon on the screen. You can also use the controls on the screen to pause, resume, rewind, fast forward, or adjust the volume of the video.

- To view more details about a photo or video, swipe up on the screen. You can see the file name, size, date, location, and other information. You can also add or edit the title, description, or tags of the photo or video.

To edit a photo or a video, follow these steps:

- Open the Gallery app and tap the photo or video you want to edit.

- Tap the Edit icon at the bottom of the screen. You can see the editing tools at the bottom of the screen, such as crop, rotate, filter, adjust, and more. You can also tap the More icon to access more editing tools, such as stickers, text, drawing, and more.

- To use an editing tool, tap the tool you want to use and then adjust the settings and options on the screen. You can also undo or redo your changes by tapping the Undo or Redo icon at the top of the screen.

- To save your changes, tap the Save icon at the top right of the screen. You can choose to save the edited photo or video as a new file, or overwrite the original file.

To organize your photos and videos, follow these steps:

- Open the Gallery app and tap the Albums icon at the bottom of the screen. You can see all your albums organized by folders, such as Camera, Screenshots, Downloads, and more. You can also tap the Stories icon to see your photos and videos organized by events, such as trips, parties, and birthdays. You can also tap the Collections icon to see your photos and videos organized by categories, such as People, Places, and Things.

- To create a new album, story, or collection, tap the Plus icon at the top right of the screen. You can enter a name for your album, story, or collection, and then select the photos and videos you want to add. Tap Create to create your album, story, or collection.

- To view an album, story, or collection, tap the album, story, or collection you want to view. You can also swipe left or right on the screen to view the previous or next album, story, or collection.

- To edit an album, story, or collection, tap the Menu icon at the top right of the screen and then tap Edit. You can rename, delete, or share your album, story, or collection. You can also add, remove, or reorder your photos and videos in your album, story, or collection. Tap Done to apply the changes.

- **Playing music and videos with the media player**

You can use the Media Player app to play music and videos on your Galaxy S24. You can also use the media player to create and manage playlists, adjust the sound quality and effects, and control the playback with gestures and voice commands. You can also sync your music and videos with Samsung Cloud or Google Drive, and stream them with other apps and devices.

To play music or a video, follow these steps:

- Open the Media Player app and tap the Music icon or the Video icon at the bottom of the screen. You can see all your music or videos organized by folders, such as Artists, Albums, Genres, and more.

- To play a song or a video, tap the song or video you want to play. You can also swipe left or right on the screen to play the previous or next song or video.

- To pause or resume the playback, tap the Pause icon or the Play icon on the screen. You can also use the controls on the screen to skip, rewind, fast forward, or adjust the volume of the song or video. You can also use the voice control feature to pause, resume, skip, rewind, or fast forward the song or video by saying voice commands, such as "Pause", "Play", "Next", "Previous", "Rewind", or "Fast forward".

- To view more options, tap the Menu icon at the top right of the screen. You can access more features, such as adding the song or video to a playlist, sharing the song or video with other apps or devices, setting the song as a ringtone or an alarm, or viewing the song or video details.

To create and manage playlists, follow these steps:

- Open the Media Player app and tap the Music icon or the Video icon at the bottom of the screen.

- To create a new playlist, tap the Plus icon at the top right of the screen. You can enter a name for your playlist, and then select the songs or videos you want to add. Tap Create to create your playlist.

- To view your playlists, tap the Playlists icon at the bottom of the screen. You can see all your playlists organized by folders, such as Recently added, Most played, Favorites, and more.

- To play a playlist, tap the playlist you want to play. You can also swipe left or right on the screen to play the previous or next playlist.

- To edit a playlist, tap the Menu icon at the top right of the screen and then tap Edit. You can rename, delete, or share your playlist. You can also add, remove, or reorder your songs or videos in your playlist. Tap Done to apply the changes.

- **Streaming music and videos with the online services**

You can use various online services to stream music and videos on your Galaxy S24. You can download and install these services from the Play Store or the Galaxy Store, such as Spotify, YouTube, Netflix, and more. You can also sync your accounts and preferences across these services, and customize the service settings and features, such as notifications, themes, and data usage.

To use an online service, follow these steps:

- Open the Play Store or the Galaxy Store app and search for the service you want to use. You can also browse the categories or recommendations to find the service you want.

- Tap the service you want to use and then tap Install to download and install the service on your device. You may need to grant some permissions and accept some terms and conditions to use the service.

- Open the service and sign in to your account or create a new one. You may need to enter your email address, password, or other information to verify your identity. You can also sign in with your Google or Facebook account if the service supports it.

- To use the service, follow the service's instructions and features. You can usually stream music and videos from various genres, artists, channels, and categories. You can also create or join playlists, stories, and live streams. You can also like, comment, share, and follow other users and content.

- To manage your service settings and features, tap the Menu icon or the Settings icon in the service. You can change various settings and features, such as notifications, themes, privacy, security, data usage, and more.

PERSONALIZATION

Your Samsung Galaxy S24 lets you personalize your device to suit your preferences and style. You can change the wallpaper and themes, the font size and style, the sound and vibration settings, the display and brightness settings, and the language and input settings. In this section, we will explain how to use these personalization features on your Galaxy S24, such as:

- Changing the wallpaper and themes
- Changing the font size and style
- Changing the sound and vibration settings
- Changing the display and brightness settings
- Changing the language and input settings

- **Changing the wallpaper and themes**

You can change the wallpaper and themes of your Galaxy S24 to customize the look and feel of your device. You can choose from the preloaded wallpapers and themes, or download and install more wallpapers and themes from the Galaxy Store or the Theme Store. You can also use your own photos or images as wallpapers or themes.

To change the wallpaper, follow these steps:

- Open the Settings app and tap Wallpaper and themes.

- Tap Wallpaper to access the wallpaper settings. You can see the available wallpapers at the bottom of the screen, such as My wallpapers, Gallery, Live wallpapers, and more. You can also tap the Explore icon to access more wallpapers from the Galaxy Store or the Theme Store.

- Tap the wallpaper you want to use, or tap the Plus icon to select your own photo or image from the gallery or the cloud. You can also apply different effects and filters to the wallpaper.

- Tap Set as wallpaper to apply the changes. You can choose to set the wallpaper for the home screen, the lock screen, or both.

To change the theme, follow these steps:

- Open the Settings app and tap Wallpaper and themes.

- Tap Themes to access the theme settings. You can see the available themes at the bottom of the screen, such as My themes, Default, Dark mode, and more. You can also tap the Explore icon to access more themes from the Galaxy Store or the Theme Store.
- Tap the theme you want to use, or tap the Plus icon to create your own theme from

your photos or images. You can also preview the theme before applying it.

- Tap Apply to apply the changes. You can choose to apply the theme for the icons, the wallpapers, the fonts, and the sounds.

ADVANCED FEATURES

Your Samsung Galaxy S24 lets you use various advanced features that enhance your productivity, creativity, and convenience. You can use the AI features and Bixby assistant to perform tasks and get information with your voice, gestures, or camera. You can use the Live Translate and Chat Assist features to communicate with people who speak different languages. You can use the Note Assist and Samsung Notes features to take notes and draw sketches with the S Pen. You can use the DeX and wireless projection features to connect your device to a larger screen and use it like a PC. You can use the wireless charging and reverse wireless charging features to charge your device or other devices without cables.

In this section, we will explain how to use these advanced features on your Galaxy S24, such as:

- Using the AI features and Bixby assistant
- Using the Live Translate and Chat Assist features
- Using the Note Assist and Samsung Notes features
- Using the DeX and wireless projection features
- Using the wireless charging and reverse wireless charging features

- **Using the AI features and Bixby assistant**

You can use the AI features and Bixby assistant to perform tasks and get information with your voice, gestures, or camera. AI stands for artificial intelligence, which is a technology that enables your device to learn from your usage patterns and preferences, and provide you with personalized and intelligent services. Bixby is a virtual assistant that lets you control your device and apps with your voice, and provides you with useful information and suggestions.

To use the AI features and Bixby assistant, follow these steps:

- Open the Settings app and tap Advanced features.

- Tap Bixby Routines to access the Bixby Routines settings. You can enable or disable the Bixby Routines feature, which automatically adjusts your device settings and runs apps based on your routines and situations. You can choose from the preloaded routines, or create your own routines by selecting the conditions and actions. You can also view and manage your routine history and recommendations.

- Tap Bixby Vision to access the Bixby Vision settings. You can enable or disable the Bixby Vision feature, which lets you use your camera to scan and recognize objects, texts, QR codes, and more. You can also choose which Bixby Vision modes to use, such as Shopping, Text, Image, Food, and more. You can also manage your Bixby Vision history and preferences.

- Tap Bixby Voice to access the Bixby Voice settings. You can enable or disable the Bixby Voice feature, which lets you use your voice to control your device and apps. You can also choose how to wake up Bixby, such as by saying "Hi Bixby", or by pressing and holding the Power button or the Bixby button. You can also manage your Bixby Voice language, voice, feedback, and history.

- To use Bixby Routines, follow the instructions on the screen to set up your routines. You can see your active routines on the notification panel or the lock screen.

You can also tap the Bixby Routines icon to access more options, such as editing, disabling, or deleting your routines.

- To use Bixby Vision, open the Camera app or the Gallery app and tap the Bixby Vision icon. You can also press and hold the Power button or the Bixby button and say "Bixby Vision". Point your camera at the object, text, QR code, or anything you want to scan and recognize. You can also select a photo or video from the gallery to scan and recognize. You can see the Bixby Vision results and suggestions on the screen, such as shopping, translating, searching, and more.

- To use Bixby Voice, press and hold the Power button or the Bixby button, or say "Hi Bixby". You can also swipe right on the home screen to access the Bixby Home, and then tap the Microphone icon. Say the command or the question you want to perform or ask, such as "Call mom", "Play music", "What's the weather today?", and more. You can also use the Quick commands feature to create your own voice commands that can perform multiple actions at once. You can see the Bixby Voice response and feedback on the screen, or hear it from the speaker or the earphone.

TROUBLESHOOTING

Your Samsung Galaxy S24 lets you troubleshoot various issues and problems that may occur on your device. You can use the safe mode, the factory reset, the Find My Mobile, and the Samsung support and service center features to fix your device and restore its functionality. In this section, we will explain how to use these troubleshooting features on your Galaxy S24, such as:

- Restarting the device in safe mode
- Resetting the device to factory settings
- Finding the device with Find My Mobile
- Contacting Samsung support and service center

- **Restarting the device in safe mode**

You can restart your device in safe mode to diagnose and fix issues caused by third-party apps or services. Safe mode disables all the apps and services that are not preloaded on your device, and allows you to uninstall or disable the problematic apps or services. You can exit the safe mode by restarting your device normally.

To restart your device in safe mode, follow these steps:

- Press and hold the Power button until the power menu appears on the screen.

- Tap and hold the Power off option until the Safe mode option appears on the screen.

- Tap Safe mode to confirm. Your device will restart in safe mode. You will see a Safe mode icon on the status bar when you are in safe mode.

- To uninstall or disable a problematic app or service, open the Settings app and tap Apps. Tap the app or service you want to uninstall or disable, and then tap Uninstall or Disable. You may need to tap the Menu icon to access these options.

- To exit the safe mode, press and hold the Power button until the power menu appears on the screen. Tap Restart to confirm. Your device will restart normally.

- **Resetting the device to factory settings**

You can reset your device to factory settings to erase all your personal data and settings, and restore your device to its original state. Factory reset is a drastic measure that should only be used as a last resort, when you cannot fix your device by any other means. Factory reset will delete all your photos, videos, music, contacts, messages, apps, and more. You should back up your data before performing a factory reset.

To reset your device to factory settings, follow these steps:

- Open the Settings app and tap General management.

- Tap Reset and then tap Factory data reset. You can see the data and settings that will be erased from your device.

- Tap Reset to confirm. You may need to enter your PIN, password, or pattern to proceed. You may also need to enter your Samsung account or Google account credentials to verify your identity.

- Tap Delete all to confirm. Your device will erase all your data and settings, and restart as a new device. You will need to set up your device again as if it was new.

- **Finding the device with Find My Mobile**

You can use the Find My Mobile feature to locate, lock, or erase your lost or stolen device. Find My Mobile is a service that allows you to remotely access and control your device using another device or a web browser. You can also use Find My Mobile to back up your data, ring your device, or send a message to your device.

To use the Find My Mobile feature, follow these steps:

- Open the Settings app and tap Biometrics and security.

- Tap Find My Mobile and then tap the switch to turn it on. You may need to sign in to your Samsung account or create a new one to use this feature. You may also need to grant some permissions and accept some terms and conditions to use this feature.

- To find your device, open another device or a web browser and go to [findmymobile.samsung.com](^1^). Sign in to your Samsung account and select your device from the list. You can see the location of your device on the map, and access various options, such as:

- Ring: You can make your device ring at full volume for one minute, even if it is in silent or vibration mode. This can help you find your device if it is nearby.

- Lock: You can lock your device with a PIN, password, or pattern, and display a message or a phone number on the lock screen. This can help you protect your data and contact information if your device is lost or stolen.

- Erase: You can erase all your data and settings from your device, and reset it to factory settings. This can help you prevent unauthorized access to your data if your device is lost or stolen. However, this will also disable the Find My Mobile feature, and you will not be able to locate or control your device anymore.

- Back up: You can back up your data from your device to Samsung Cloud or Google Drive. This can help you restore your data if you lose your device or perform a factory reset.

- Retrieve calls/messages: You can retrieve the recent call logs and messages from your device. This can help you check if anyone has used your device or contacted you.

- Extend battery life: You can extend the battery life of your device by turning on the power saving mode. This can help you locate your device for a longer time if it has a low battery.

- **Contacting Samsung support and service center**

You can contact Samsung support and service center to get help and assistance with your device. Samsung support and service center can provide you with technical support, warranty service, repair service, and more. You can contact Samsung support and service center by phone, chat, email, or visit.

To contact Samsung support and service center, follow these steps:

- Open the Settings app and tap About phone.

- Tap Contact us to access the contact options. You can choose from the following options, depending on your region and availability.

- Phone: You can call the Samsung customer service number to speak with a representative. You can also request a callback from Samsung, or schedule a call for a later time.

- Chat: You can chat with a Samsung expert online, using text or video. You can also share your screen with the Samsung expert to show your issue or problem.

- Email: You can send an email to Samsung with your question or feedback. You can also attach files or screenshots to your email. You will receive a reply from Samsung within 24 hours.

- Visit: You can visit a Samsung service center near you to get your device checked, repaired, or replaced. You can also book an appointment online to save your time and avoid waiting in line.